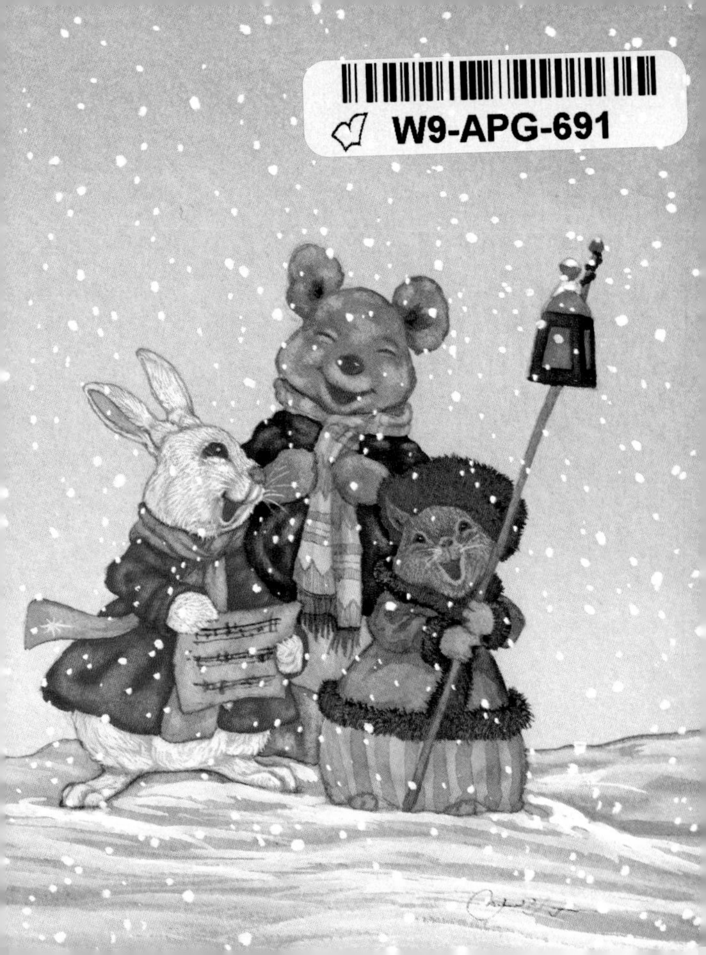

This book brings you
glad tidings for Christmas
and a happy New Year

T O

. . . .

F R O M

. . . .

We Wish You a Merry Christmas

ILLUSTRATED BY

Michael Hague

Henry Holt and Company

NEW YORK

*W*e wish you a merry Christmas,

we wish you a merry Christmas,

we wish you a merry Christmas

and a happy New Year!

*G*lad tidings we bring

to you and your kin,

*G*lad tidings for Christmas

and a happy New Year!

*P*lease bring us some figgy pudding,

Please bring us some figgy pudding,

*P*lease bring us some figgy pudding,

and bring it right now!

*W*e won't go until we get some,

We won't go until we get some,

*W*e won't go until we get some,

so bring it right now!

*W*e wish you a merry Christmas,

we wish you a merry Christmas,

we wish you a

Merry Christmas

and a

Happy New Year!

Published by Henry Holt and Company, Inc., 115 West 18th Street, New York, New York 10011.

Published in Canada by Fitzhenry & Whiteside Limited, 195 Allstate Parkway, Markham, Ontario L3R 4T8.

Library of Congress Cataloging-in-Publication Data

Hague, Michael.

We wish you a Merry Christmas / illustrated by Michael Hague.

Summary: An illustrated edition of the traditional Christmas carol.

ISBN 0-8050-1006-8

1. Carols, English—Juvenile literature. 2. Christmas music—Juvenile literature.

3. Folk-songs, English—Juvenile literature.

[1. Carols, English. 2. Christmas music. 3. Folk songs, English.] I. Title.

PZ8.3.H11935We 1990

782.42'1723—dc20   90-32067

Henry Holt books are available at special discounts for bulk purchases for sales promotions, premiums, fund-raising, or educational use. Special editions or book excerpts can also be created to specification. For details contact:
Special Sales Director, Henry Holt & Co., Inc., 115 West 18th Street, New York, New York 10011.

First Edition | Designed by Marc Cheshire

Printed in the United States of America

Recognizing the importance of preserving the written word,
Henry Holt and Company, Inc., by policy, prints all
of its first editions on acid-free paper.

1 3 5 7 9 10 8 6 4 2